Meta's MovieGen
The AI Revolution Transforming Video Creation

Why Filmmakers and Creators Can't Overlook the Next Generation of Artificial Intelligence-Enhanced Content

Alejandro S. Diego

Copyright © Alejandro S. Diego, 2024.

All rights reserved. No part of this publication may be reproduced, distributed, or transmitted in any form or by any means, including photocopying, recording, or other electronic or mechanical methods, without the prior written permission of the publisher, except in the case of brief quotations embodied in critical reviews and certain other noncommercial uses permitted by copyright law.

Table of Contents

Introduction 3
Chapter 1: Unveiling Meta's MovieGen 6
Chapter 2: The Key Features of Meta's MovieGen .. 12
Chapter 3: Pushing the Boundaries of Realism in Video 19
Chapter 4: MovieGen in Action: Showcasing Versatility 29
Chapter 5: The Power of Text-to-Video Transformation 41
Chapter 6: Personalization and Generative Video Effects 53
Chapter 7: Video-to-Audio: The Sound Revolution. 65
Chapter 8: What MovieGen Means for Filmmakers and Creators 77
Chapter 9: The Future of Video Creation with AI 93
Chapter 10: Preparing for the AI-Driven Future 109
Conclusion 124

Introduction

Artificial intelligence has emerged as one of the most transformative technologies of the modern era, finding applications across a wide range of industries. From healthcare to finance, AI has rapidly evolved, becoming integral to solving complex problems and automating processes that were once thought to be exclusively within the realm of human expertise. In industries like automotive manufacturing, retail, and even creative fields such as music composition and visual arts, AI has demonstrated its versatility by streamlining workflows, enhancing precision, and introducing new possibilities for innovation. Yet, one of the most exciting areas where AI is now making an unprecedented impact is video creation, where it is revolutionizing how we think about and produce visual media.

Meta, a company already recognized for its advancements in social media and virtual reality, has taken a surprising lead in AI-driven video creation. For many, Meta's entry into this field was unexpected, especially considering the dominance of other tech giants focused specifically on AI-powered tools. However, with the introduction of MovieGen, Meta has positioned itself at the forefront of this rapidly evolving sector. MovieGen is more than just a tool for video generation; it represents a leap in how artificial intelligence can be harnessed to transform simple text into high-quality, visually immersive content. This innovation showcases Meta's ability to not only compete but also exceed expectations in a field where creativity and technology intersect.

The purpose of this book is to explore the remarkable capabilities of Meta's MovieGen and its potential to reshape the landscape of video creation. By delving into the technology behind MovieGen and examining its broader implications for filmmakers, content creators, and visual media as a whole, this book aims to provide a comprehensive understanding of how AI is driving the future of storytelling. Meta's leadership in AI, particularly in video creation, is poised to redefine the boundaries of what is possible, making it an essential tool for anyone involved in the world of digital content.

Chapter 1: Unveiling Meta's MovieGen

Meta's journey into the world of AI-driven video creation has been a gradual yet groundbreaking evolution. The company, originally known for its dominance in social media through platforms like Facebook and Instagram, soon expanded its focus to include artificial intelligence, recognizing the immense potential AI had to offer across multiple fields. Over the years, Meta has invested heavily in AI research, leading to the development of advanced technologies that not only enhance user experience but also push the boundaries of what AI can achieve. One of the most notable steps in this direction was Meta's development of LLaMA (Large Language Model Meta AI), a language model designed to handle complex language tasks with remarkable accuracy. This success in AI language models laid the groundwork for Meta to explore other areas, including visual media.

The introduction of MovieGen marked a pivotal moment in Meta's journey. As the company ventured into video generation, it wasn't just following the trends—it was setting new ones. MovieGen stands as a testament to Meta's capability to integrate cutting-edge AI into creative processes, offering an unprecedented tool for video production. This system allows users to generate detailed and highly realistic videos from simple text descriptions, blurring the lines between human creativity and machine intelligence. It leverages advanced AI models to interpret textual prompts and transform them into visually rich scenes, complete with accurate lighting, realistic physics, and intricate details that would have otherwise required extensive manual effort.

What makes MovieGen particularly significant is its role in the larger AI landscape. As many tech companies focus on developing specialized tools for specific tasks, Meta has shown its ability to create versatile systems that span multiple domains. MovieGen not only competes with other video generation models but often surpasses them in terms of realism and efficiency. The technology behind it has implications that extend far beyond entertainment; it has the potential to revolutionize industries such as marketing, education, and even virtual reality, where the creation of immersive environments is becoming increasingly important. In this context, MovieGen is not just a tool—it is a pioneering innovation that signifies Meta's leadership in the AI revolution.

The launch of MovieGen sent shockwaves through the AI community, catching many experts by surprise. While Meta had already established itself as a key player in the tech space, its focus on AI-driven video creation was relatively unexpected. The company had been known for projects like LLaMA and its ventures into virtual reality, but few anticipated that Meta would introduce a video generation system that could compete—and, in some cases, outperform—existing platforms specifically designed for such tasks. MovieGen's emergence quickly drew attention, not just because of its impressive capabilities, but because it challenged the established hierarchy of AI video generation technologies.

When MovieGen was first introduced, its ability to convert simple text into highly detailed and visually accurate videos astounded many in the AI field. Experts had grown accustomed to seeing advancements in text-based models and image generation, but video creation was still a complex frontier. The intricacies involved in generating video—where factors like lighting, motion, and physics must interact seamlessly—posed significant challenges even for the most advanced AI systems. Meta's ability to overcome these challenges and present a tool capable of producing high-quality, realistic video content left many in the industry wondering how they had managed to achieve such a breakthrough in such a short period of time.

Comparisons were quickly drawn between MovieGen and other major systems, most notably Runway Gen 3 Alpha, which had been considered one of the top players in AI-driven video creation. Runway Gen 3 Alpha had earned its place by delivering impressive results in video generation, particularly in creative fields like digital art and filmmaking. However, MovieGen set itself apart by outperforming Runway Gen 3 Alpha in several key areas. For instance, MovieGen demonstrated a superior ability to manage complex lighting scenarios and handle dynamic movement with greater fluidity, something that many AI models struggled with. The seamless integration of physics and visual effects, such as reflections and shadows, made MovieGen's output appear more realistic and immersive compared to other systems.

The initial reactions within the AI community reflected a mix of awe and curiosity. How had Meta, a company whose primary reputation lay in social media and virtual reality, managed to leap ahead of specialized AI firms in the video generation space? This development forced many experts to reevaluate Meta's position in the AI world, recognizing that the company was not just following trends but actively pushing the envelope of what AI could accomplish. MovieGen's debut effectively positioned Meta as a leader in the AI revolution, capable of competing with—and sometimes surpassing—companies that had previously been seen as frontrunners in AI-driven creative tools.

Chapter 2: The Key Features of Meta's MovieGen

At the heart of Meta's MovieGen is its impressive 30 billion parameter model, which serves as the engine behind its remarkable ability to generate highly realistic videos from text descriptions. This enormous parameter count allows the system to process and understand intricate details within the input, enabling it to generate visuals that are not only coherent but also rich in detail. Parameters in AI models refer to the weights and biases that the model uses to make predictions and decisions, and having 30 billion of these parameters means that MovieGen can capture a vast range of subtleties, from texture and lighting to motion and depth perception, making the resulting video content exceptionally lifelike.

What sets MovieGen apart is its ability to break down complex visual scenes and translate them into pixel-perfect representations. The model can handle challenging elements such as the interplay between light and shadow, the motion of objects in space, and even the way surfaces reflect or absorb light. These aspects of video generation have historically been difficult for AI to master, particularly when multiple dynamic elements are involved. However, MovieGen's advanced architecture allows it to manage these tasks seamlessly, producing videos that rival what humans can create through manual animation or video editing.

In addition to the visual generation capabilities of MovieGen, Meta introduced MovieGen Audio, a complementary 13 billion parameter model designed specifically to enhance video sound. Sound is an essential element in creating an immersive viewing experience, and Meta recognized that simply generating high-quality video wasn't enough—audio needed to match the visuals in realism and coherence. MovieGen Audio achieves this by generating sound effects, ambient noise, and other audio elements that correspond to the actions and environments in the generated video.

For example, if MovieGen generates a scene of a car driving down a street, MovieGen Audio can accurately produce the sound of the car engine, the tires on the road, and the background noise of a bustling city. The audio model analyzes the visual inputs and predicts the types of sounds that should accompany each action, adding depth and realism to the final output. This ability to synchronize sound with visual elements is particularly important for applications like film production, gaming, and virtual reality, where both sight and sound are critical to delivering a fully immersive experience.

By combining the power of its 30 billion parameter visual model with the precision of MovieGen Audio, Meta has created a system that not only generates stunning video but also provides the soundscape needed to bring those videos to life. The result is a platform that offers creators a comprehensive solution for generating content that feels authentic, whether it's for professional use or entertainment.

One of the standout features of MovieGen is its ability to personalize video creation and editing, which opens up new possibilities for content creators. At its core, MovieGen's personalized video model allows users to input their own images or footage, which the AI then adapts and integrates into entirely new video content. This level of customization means that creators can not only generate videos from scratch but also tailor them to specific themes, styles, or even personal preferences, making the system an incredibly versatile tool for anyone working in digital media.

MovieGen's personalized video model works by analyzing the input image or video provided by the user and then generating a new, coherent scene around it. For instance, a user can upload a single image of a person, and MovieGen will create a personalized video that incorporates the visual style and details of that image, allowing for the creation of tailored content that feels unique and specific to the user's needs. The system can adapt the image into different settings, actions, or scenarios, making it ideal for content creators looking to develop personalized videos for social media, advertising, or personal projects.

In terms of editing capabilities, MovieGen takes things a step further by offering tools that allow users to make dynamic adjustments to their videos after generation. For example, the post-training extensions of the model enable video editing functions such as adding new elements, changing environments, or even modifying the appearance of characters within the scene. These capabilities give creators significant control over the final product, allowing for iterative adjustments without the need to manually recreate the entire video.

A real-world application of this personalized video model is in the marketing and advertising sector, where businesses often need to create targeted content for different audiences. With MovieGen, marketers can quickly generate personalized video ads that align with specific consumer profiles, adjusting the visual elements and messaging for different demographics. This can save time and resources while still delivering highly engaging content that resonates with the target audience.

Another example comes from the world of social media content creation, where influencers and creators constantly need fresh, engaging material to stay relevant. With MovieGen, they can personalize videos based on their brand, aesthetic, or even their followers' preferences, ensuring that each piece of content feels authentic and unique. Furthermore, the system's editing capabilities allow for on-the-fly adjustments, meaning creators can easily modify videos based on feedback or trends without having to start from scratch.

In professional filmmaking, MovieGen's personalized video creation can serve as a valuable tool during pre-visualization stages, where directors can input basic concepts or still images and have the system generate dynamic scenes for review. This allows filmmakers to experiment with different visual styles, settings, and character actions before committing to full production, providing a low-cost way to test ideas and refine concepts.

By offering a blend of personalized video creation and powerful editing capabilities, MovieGen presents significant advantages to creators across industries. Whether used for marketing, content creation, or even professional filmmaking, the system empowers users to take control of their creative process, generating videos that are both tailored to specific needs and easy to refine. This flexibility is one of the key factors that sets MovieGen apart, making it an invaluable tool for anyone looking to harness the power of AI in their video production efforts.

Chapter 3: Pushing the Boundaries of Realism in Video

One of the most remarkable aspects of MovieGen's technology is its ability to handle lighting, physics, and detail precision, making the AI-generated videos not only visually impressive but also highly realistic. These elements are crucial in video generation because they influence how viewers perceive depth, movement, and overall authenticity. MovieGen's advanced algorithms manage to capture the subtleties of light interaction and physical dynamics in ways that were previously difficult for AI models to achieve, marking a significant leap forward in AI-driven video creation.

In terms of lighting, MovieGen excels at understanding how light behaves in different environments and how it interacts with various surfaces and objects. This is a complex task because light can affect multiple elements in a scene simultaneously—casting shadows, reflecting off shiny surfaces, and diffusing through translucent materials. What sets MovieGen apart is its ability to calculate these light dynamics with a high degree of accuracy, ensuring that every shadow, reflection, and light source is consistent with the environment and action taking place.

For instance, in the case of the fire dancing scene generated by MovieGen, the system had to manage a variety of lighting challenges. Fire is a dynamic light source, constantly flickering and casting moving shadows. In this scene, the AI accurately rendered how the flames illuminated the dancer's body, reflecting the warm glow of the fire onto his skin and the surrounding ground. The light from the fire changed depending on the dancer's movements, casting longer or shorter shadows based on his position and motion. MovieGen also captured how the fire's light interacted with the background environment, ensuring that every reflection and shadow behaved as it would in a real-world scenario. This level of precision in lighting gives the scene a tangible sense of realism, making the viewer feel as if they are watching a live performance rather than an AI-generated video.

Physics is another area where MovieGen shows its technical prowess. Handling movement and interaction between objects in a realistic way is one of the biggest challenges in video generation. MovieGen's algorithms are capable of simulating the physical properties of objects, such as gravity, motion, and the way surfaces react when coming into contact with other elements. This is particularly evident in another example: the tropical sloth video. In this scene, a sloth is depicted lounging on a floating donut in a pool, holding a tropical drink. As the sloth shifts on the inflatable, MovieGen accurately reflects how the water moves in response, creating ripples that spread out across the pool. The movement of the sloth's body also causes subtle changes in the water's reflection, demonstrating the AI's ability to manage both large-scale and small-scale physical interactions simultaneously.

Beyond the realistic water dynamics, the sloth's sunglasses cast accurate shadows based on the direction of sunlight, while reflections on the water's surface change with the sloth's movements. The interplay between light and water in this scene demonstrates MovieGen's ability to simulate complex environments where multiple elements must interact seamlessly. The physics of the water, the sloth's movement, and the behavior of light all come together to create a scene that is visually convincing and incredibly detailed.

These case studies highlight just how advanced MovieGen is in handling lighting and physics. The fire dancing scene shows the system's mastery of dynamic lighting, while the tropical sloth example showcases its capability in managing both physics and detail precision. Together, they illustrate how MovieGen's technical advancements are setting a new standard for AI-generated video content. By accurately simulating how light behaves and how objects interact in physical spaces, MovieGen achieves a level of realism that brings AI-generated videos closer to the quality of professionally produced, human-made content.

AI video generation has traditionally faced significant challenges when it comes to creating visually realistic content. Some of the most persistent issues involve handling lighting, reflections, and physics in a way that mirrors real-world behavior. These elements are complex to simulate because they require an AI model to account for numerous variables simultaneously, all of which interact dynamically within a scene. Achieving this level of detail has historically been a stumbling block for many AI systems, often resulting in videos that feel artificial, flat, or disjointed. However, MovieGen has made substantial strides in overcoming these obstacles, setting it apart from earlier models and competitors in the space.

One of the primary difficulties in AI video generation is accurately simulating lighting.

Lighting is a constantly shifting variable that influences the mood, depth, and realism of a scene. In previous AI models, light sources often appeared static or unconvincing, casting unrealistic shadows or failing to interact properly with reflective surfaces. For example, in scenes where multiple light sources are present, such as sunlight, lamps, or fire, the AI would struggle to manage how these lights interact with objects and each other. This could lead to glaring issues, like shadows being cast in the wrong direction or inconsistent reflections that disrupt the viewer's sense of immersion.

MovieGen addresses this challenge by employing sophisticated algorithms that simulate lighting in a dynamic, responsive way. The system can calculate the direction, intensity, and diffusion of light based on the scene's context, ensuring that each light source behaves as it would in the real world. For instance, in scenes where light reflects off water or metallic surfaces, MovieGen accurately captures how those reflections change based on the viewer's perspective and the movement within the video. This ability to render light interactions correctly plays a key role in making the generated videos feel more lifelike.

Reflections are another significant challenge in AI video generation, especially when objects of varying textures and materials are present in the same scene. Reflective surfaces, such as water, glass, or shiny metals, require the AI to calculate how these materials bounce light and create visual echoes of their surroundings. Many AI models have struggled with this because reflections demand precise calculations that vary depending on the angle, intensity of light, and the nature of the reflective surface. Poorly generated reflections can immediately break the illusion of realism, drawing attention to the artificiality of the video.

MovieGen excels in handling reflections by leveraging its powerful 30 billion parameter model, which gives it the capacity to process intricate visual details. Whether reflecting the sky on the surface of a pool or rendering the subtle gleam of light off a metallic object, MovieGen manages to produce reflections that are not only accurate but also dynamic, adjusting seamlessly as objects and light sources shift within the frame. This ensures that scenes featuring reflective surfaces remain coherent and visually convincing, further enhancing the overall realism of the generated content.

Physics is another area where AI models typically encounter difficulties. Simulating real-world physics, such as gravity, motion, and object interactions, is crucial for making animated or generated content feel authentic. Earlier AI models often fell short in this domain, resulting in awkward object movements or incorrect interactions that disrupted the flow of the scene. For example, AI-generated videos might show objects floating unnaturally, colliding in ways that defy the laws of physics, or failing to respond to environmental factors like wind or water.

MovieGen's approach to physics is one of its most significant advancements. The system carefully calculates how objects should move and interact with their environment, whether it's the way ripples form when something moves in water or how an object casts a shadow as it changes position. By applying realistic physical dynamics to these elements, MovieGen creates scenes where movements feel natural, adding to the believability of the video. This is especially important in videos where multiple objects are in motion or interacting, as these dynamics need to be synchronized to maintain coherence.

In sum, MovieGen's ability to address the common struggles of lighting, reflections, and physics in AI video generation has set it apart from earlier models and competitors. By creating highly realistic videos that manage these complex elements with precision, MovieGen has bridged the gap between AI-generated content and human-made production quality. These advancements are key to the system's success, providing creators with a tool that generates content indistinguishable from reality, pushing the boundaries of what AI in video production can achieve.

Chapter 4: MovieGen in Action: Showcasing Versatility

In one of MovieGen's more playful yet technically impressive examples, a sloth wearing pink sunglasses lounges on a donut float in a tropical pool. While the scene may seem lighthearted, it serves as a striking demonstration of the AI's ability to manage complex visual details like reflections and shadows. The sloth itself, wearing oversized pink sunglasses, provides a perfect opportunity to test how MovieGen handles the interaction between light and reflective surfaces. The glasses, a prominent feature, cast subtle yet accurate reflections of the surrounding environment. As sunlight hits the sunglasses, MovieGen carefully calculates how the reflections of the water, sky, and surrounding foliage should appear on the lenses. This precise handling of reflections ensures that the glasses do not simply act as static, flat objects, but instead reflect light and shadow in a dynamic and lifelike manner.

Beyond the reflections in the sunglasses, the sloth's positioning on the donut float creates another challenge for accurate shadow rendering. As the sloth moves slightly on the inflatable, the shadows it casts on the surface of the water and on the float itself change accordingly. MovieGen's ability to adapt these shadows in real-time is critical for maintaining the believability of the scene. The subtle movement of the float on the water adds another layer of complexity, as the AI must calculate how the sunlight interacts with both the sloth and the rippling water underneath. Shadows shift and dance as the float gently rocks, and MovieGen's attention to these small details contributes to a sense of realism that can often be lacking in AI-generated content.

The water's surface itself is also a key player in the scene's realism. MovieGen demonstrates its mastery over reflections here by simulating how the sunlight interacts with the gently rippling water. The reflection of the sloth and the float on the water is rendered with impressive accuracy, constantly changing as the water moves. Even the sloth's sunglasses, a smaller reflective surface, are mirrored on the water's surface, albeit in a more distorted and subtle manner due to the ripples. This attention to the nuances of how light interacts with reflective surfaces is a hallmark of MovieGen's technological capabilities, making what could have been a simple scene feel immersive and lifelike.

Another notable example is the video of a red-faced monkey sitting in a natural hot spring, playing with a miniature wooden sailboat. This scene is a masterclass in water dynamics and reflections, showcasing how MovieGen manages the complex interplay of light, water, and motion. The hot spring, surrounded by lush greenery and rocks, provides a visually rich environment filled with reflective surfaces and moving water, both of which pose significant challenges for any AI video generation system.

In this example, the water's movement is key to the scene's realism. As the monkey gently interacts with the boat, small ripples form and spread across the surface of the water. MovieGen's handling of these ripples is remarkably accurate, demonstrating a deep understanding of how water behaves in response to motion. The ripples not only respond to the monkey's movements but also interact with the reflection of the boat, distorting it in a way that feels natural and convincing. This small but important detail brings the scene to life, as the reflections in the water shift and change with the movement of both the monkey and the boat.

Moreover, the monkey's reflection on the water is handled with impressive precision. The AI accurately captures how the monkey's image is mirrored in the stiller parts of the water while being gently distorted in the areas where ripples occur. The reflections of the surrounding greenery and rocks also contribute to the overall sense of depth in the scene. As the water moves, these reflections shift and blur, creating a realistic interaction between the environment and the water's surface.

The physical interaction between the boat and the water is another standout feature. As the boat floats on the hot spring, MovieGen ensures that the physics governing its movement are consistent with real-world behavior. The boat bobs gently on the surface, reacting to both the monkey's touch and the natural movement of the water. The way the miniature sail and rudder respond to the water's movement, swaying gently, adds an extra layer of detail that reinforces the realism of the scene.

These two examples—the sloth with pink sunglasses and the monkey in the hot spring—highlight MovieGen's ability to handle reflections, shadows, and water dynamics with extraordinary accuracy. By mastering these complex visual details, MovieGen creates videos that feel immersive and real, even when the scenes themselves are whimsical or imaginative. The precision with which the AI manages light, shadow, and motion across different surfaces is what sets it apart from other AI video generation systems, allowing creators to produce content that rivals what could be achieved through traditional means of filmmaking or animation.

MovieGen stands out in the world of AI-generated content due to its exceptional handling of physics and visual consistency, both of which contribute to a level of realism that is rare in AI-driven video production. One of the key reasons MovieGen succeeds in creating such lifelike videos is its ability to simulate real-world physical laws and maintain visual coherence across various elements in a scene. Whether it's the interaction between objects, the behavior of light, or the motion of characters, MovieGen's ability to replicate the complexities of the physical world is what sets it apart.

At the core of MovieGen's realism is its sophisticated approach to physics. AI video models have traditionally struggled with physical interactions, often resulting in awkward or unnatural movements that break the illusion of reality. However, MovieGen excels in this area by simulating gravity, inertia, and collision in a way that mirrors real-world behavior. For instance, when an object falls, MovieGen accurately calculates its trajectory, accounting for speed, weight, and impact, ensuring that it lands as it would in reality. This attention to the physical laws governing motion and interaction is critical in scenes where multiple objects are in motion, as any inconsistencies can quickly disrupt the viewer's sense of immersion.

A prime example of this can be seen in how MovieGen handles character movement. In many AI-generated videos, characters can appear stiff or floaty, with their movements not quite matching the environment around them. MovieGen, on the other hand, produces characters whose actions are grounded in the environment. Whether a character is walking, running, or interacting with objects, the AI ensures that their movements are fluid and that their physical interactions—like the way their feet touch the ground or how their hands grip objects—are precise. This is especially important in dynamic scenes where the motion of characters affects their surroundings, such as footsteps leaving impressions in sand or hands causing ripples in water.

The dynamic interactions between objects and their environment further demonstrate MovieGen's strengths. In scenes where multiple elements are involved, MovieGen maintains a high degree of visual consistency by accurately simulating how these elements influence each other. For example, in the tropical sloth video, the sloth's movements cause ripples in the water, and these ripples, in turn, alter the reflection of the sloth and its sunglasses on the water's surface. MovieGen's ability to manage these subtle interactions is critical for creating a cohesive scene where all elements work in harmony rather than appearing disconnected or artificial.

Another area where MovieGen shines is its handling of environmental factors like wind, water, and lighting. In the monkey hot spring scene, the system doesn't just generate static reflections or ripples—it dynamically adjusts these based on the monkey's interactions with the water. As the monkey moves the small sailboat, the ripples spread outward, distorting reflections and changing the surface of the water in real-time. This attention to environmental feedback is key to achieving realism, as it ensures that the environment responds naturally to changes within it, just as it would in the physical world.

Lighting is another aspect where MovieGen's attention to detail enhances realism. Rather than applying a single, uniform light source, the AI calculates how light interacts with different materials, surfaces, and angles. This means that objects in a scene cast appropriate shadows and reflect light in ways that are consistent with their environment. For example, in the fire dancing scene, the flickering flames cast moving shadows and illuminate the dancer's body, with the light adjusting as the dancer moves and the fire's intensity fluctuates. Such dynamic lighting effects contribute to the overall believability of the scene.

MovieGen's realism also benefits from its ability to manage complex visual details without losing coherence. In scenes involving multiple reflective or translucent surfaces—like water, glass, or shiny metals—MovieGen handles how light passes through or bounces off these materials with remarkable precision. In the sloth video, for instance, the way sunlight reflects off the pool's surface, interacts with the sloth's sunglasses, and changes depending on the angle of the viewer is executed with a level of accuracy that is rarely seen in AI-generated content. This consistency in rendering reflections, shadows, and physics across various surfaces ensures that the video remains visually coherent, regardless of how complex the scene may be.

The system's ability to maintain this high degree of realism is crucial for content creators who rely on visual accuracy to tell compelling stories or produce immersive experiences. In industries like filmmaking, advertising, or gaming, where realism can make or break a viewer's engagement, MovieGen offers a significant advantage by generating content that feels both believable and dynamic. The seamless interactions between objects and environments, coupled with precise handling of light and physics, allow creators to produce content that closely mimics what could be achieved with traditional video production methods, but with the efficiency and flexibility of AI.

In summary, MovieGen's standout feature is its ability to consistently deliver realism through accurate physics and dynamic interactions. By focusing on the intricate ways in which objects move, interact, and respond to their environments, MovieGen generates videos that feel alive and grounded in reality. This capability makes it a powerful tool for content creators seeking to push the boundaries of what AI-generated video can achieve while maintaining the level of detail and precision required for high-quality visual storytelling.

Chapter 5: The Power of Text-to-Video Transformation

MovieGen's ability to transform simple text into detailed video represents one of its most remarkable advancements. This feature allows users to input basic descriptions, which the AI then processes to generate fully realized video content. The system's power lies in its capacity to understand and interpret the nuances of text, transforming it into visual elements such as movement, lighting, physics, and environmental details. Here's a step-by-step explanation of how MovieGen turns text into compelling video.

The process begins with the text input, where a user provides a description of the scene they want to generate. This input can range from simple phrases to more detailed descriptions. For example, the user might input something like, "A man is dancing with fire in his hands, making wide circular motions. He's shirtless, with a green cloth around his waist, standing on the beach at sunset, with calm seas in the background." MovieGen processes this input and breaks it down into various components that will define the video: the characters, objects, environment, actions, and lighting conditions.

Once the text input is provided, MovieGen's model interprets the description and begins mapping out the visual elements. In the fiery dance example, for instance, the system starts by generating the character—shirtless, barefoot, with a green cloth around his waist. The AI creates the physical characteristics and attire based on the details mentioned. It also ensures that the character's movements correspond to the "wide circular motions" described in the text, capturing the fluidity and grace of the fire dance. This step is crucial because it's where the AI ensures that the character's movements match the intended action, allowing the video to have a natural flow.

The next step involves generating the environment. In the fiery dance scene, the beach at sunset with calm seas provides a specific setting for the action.

MovieGen uses the description of the beach and the sunset to simulate the lighting conditions, casting the appropriate warm glow on the dancer and the surroundings. The interaction between light and objects is carefully calculated—sunset light tends to cast long shadows and a soft, warm hue, which the AI accurately renders. The calm seas in the background also play a role in creating a serene atmosphere, which is visually translated into gentle waves and the reflective quality of the water.

Once the character and environment are mapped out, the AI focuses on the most dynamic element: the fire. Fire presents a significant challenge for any video generation system because it is constantly in motion, casting ever-changing light and shadows. MovieGen's model captures this complexity by ensuring that the flames move realistically in the dancer's hands, flickering as he makes wide circular motions. The light from the fire illuminates both the dancer and the surrounding ground, shifting and moving as the flames swirl in the air. This dynamic lighting not only enhances the realism of the video but also immerses the viewer in the scene.

In another example, where the text input describes "a girl running across a beach holding a kite," the process follows a similar pattern. First, the AI generates the girl—her appearance, her clothing (jean shorts and a yellow t-shirt), and her posture as she runs. It ensures that her movements are fluid and responsive to the environment, simulating the natural motion of running on sand, where her feet make slight impressions with each step. The AI then focuses on the kite, which is described as flying in the wind. It ensures that the kite's movements are not rigid but rather dynamic, reflecting the natural motion of something being pulled by both the girl and the wind.

The environment plays a significant role in this scene as well. The AI generates the beach, incorporating the texture of the sand, the waves gently lapping at the shore, and the bright sunlight overhead. This scene also demonstrates MovieGen's ability to handle lighting and physics. The sunlight, for instance, casts shadows as the girl runs, and the AI captures how her kite's shadow stretches across the beach. The wind, another environmental factor, interacts with both the kite and the girl's hair and clothing, creating a sense of movement that feels natural and immersive.

The final step in the process involves rendering the video in high resolution, ensuring that all the elements—characters, environment, lighting, and movement—come together cohesively. In the fiery dance example, the combination of the dancer's fluid motions, the dynamic fire, and the serene background makes for a visually compelling scene. The same can be said for the girl running with the kite, where the smoothness of her movements and the interaction between the kite, the wind, and the environment create a sense of realism.

These examples highlight MovieGen's ability to take a simple text description and transform it into a highly detailed and dynamic video. By interpreting the text input and breaking it down into visual components, MovieGen ensures that every aspect of the scene—from lighting and physics to character movement and environmental interaction—is accurately represented. This capability not only makes it a powerful tool for creators but also demonstrates the incredible potential of AI in video production, allowing users to create rich, immersive content from just a few lines of text.

The role of AI in future content creation is poised to be transformative, fundamentally changing how filmmakers and digital creators approach the creative process. As AI tools like Meta's MovieGen become more advanced and accessible, they will provide creators with new ways to conceptualize, produce, and refine content, offering a level of efficiency and flexibility that was previously unimaginable. These tools will not only streamline workflows but also allow for faster production times without sacrificing quality, enabling creators to focus more on the artistic aspects of storytelling.

One of the most significant ways AI will impact content creation is through the integration of AI-driven tools into every stage of production. Filmmakers, for example, will be able to use AI to generate pre-visualizations based on early script drafts or simple descriptions, allowing them to see how scenes might play out before full production even begins. This pre-visualization capability can help directors and cinematographers make key decisions about lighting, camera angles, and shot composition early on, ultimately saving time during the actual filming process. By offering this kind of immediate feedback, AI will allow for a more iterative and experimental approach to filmmaking, where creators can quickly test ideas and make adjustments on the fly.

In digital content creation, AI tools will offer even more possibilities. For example, social media content creators, influencers, and marketing teams will be able to generate personalized videos tailored to specific audiences with minimal effort. Instead of spending hours editing and refining content manually, creators can input basic ideas or themes, and AI systems like MovieGen will generate polished videos that fit the brand's aesthetic and message. This kind of integration will enable creators to produce high-quality content at scale, meeting the ever-increasing demands for fresh material in today's fast-paced digital landscape.

AI's ability to automate labor-intensive tasks will also be a game-changer for reducing production time. In traditional filmmaking or video production, processes like editing, rendering, and special effects often require extensive manual effort and are time-consuming. AI-driven video generation tools will be able to handle much of this workload, from automatically editing scenes based on specified parameters to generating visual effects that would typically take weeks or months to complete. This automation will not only speed up production but also reduce costs, making high-quality content creation more accessible to independent filmmakers and smaller production companies that might not have the resources of larger studios.

For larger film productions, AI tools like MovieGen will be invaluable for creating complex CGI or VFX-heavy scenes in a fraction of the time. By generating detailed, realistic video content based on text descriptions or rough models, AI can eliminate the need for extensive post-production work. Filmmakers will be able to generate high-quality visual effects on the spot, giving them more creative control during the shooting process. This could lead to faster turnaround times for movies and series, as well as greater flexibility in reshooting or adjusting scenes based on real-time feedback.

Moreover, AI tools will likely be integrated into post-production workflows, allowing editors and special effects teams to refine and enhance content more efficiently. For example, AI could be used to automatically match lighting and color tones across different shots, ensure continuity in scenes, or even generate entire sequences that would normally require manual animation or green screen work. The potential for streamlined workflows will not only reduce the time needed for post-production but also allow for a higher degree of precision in editing, ensuring that the final product aligns more closely with the creator's vision.

In addition to enhancing production efficiency, AI will open up new creative possibilities by enabling filmmakers and creators to experiment with ideas that would have been difficult or costly to achieve through traditional methods. For instance, AI-generated content could allow creators to visualize alternative storylines, generate multiple versions of the same scene, or even create entirely new worlds that would be impossible to film in real life. This creative freedom, coupled with AI's ability to generate high-quality content quickly, will push the boundaries of storytelling, giving creators the tools to bring their most ambitious ideas to life.

Looking forward, the integration of AI into content creation will likely lead to more personalized and interactive forms of entertainment. Filmmakers and digital creators will be able to tailor their content to specific audiences, generating multiple versions of the same film or video to suit different tastes, cultures, or preferences. Interactive content, where viewers can influence the direction of the story in real-time, could become a new norm, with AI-driven systems dynamically adjusting the narrative based on user input.

In conclusion, the future of content creation will be defined by the seamless integration of AI tools that enhance both the creative and technical aspects of the production process. Filmmakers and digital creators will be able to harness AI to streamline workflows, reduce production time, and open up new creative avenues, all while maintaining a high level of quality and precision. As AI continues to evolve, it will become an indispensable tool for anyone involved in visual storytelling, enabling them to produce more innovative, personalized, and immersive content than ever before.

Chapter 6: Personalization and Generative Video Effects

MovieGen's ability to expand the possibilities of personalized content is one of its most innovative features, offering content creators a powerful tool to tailor videos according to specific needs or preferences. This feature allows users to provide images that MovieGen incorporates into the video generation process, creating highly customized content that reflects the user's vision. By analyzing these user-provided images, MovieGen adapts elements such as the character design, environment, and even visual style, ensuring that the generated video aligns closely with the desired aesthetic or context.

The process begins with the user submitting one or more images that serve as references for the AI to follow. These images can depict anything from a person, an object, or a specific location, which MovieGen then uses to build a video that closely matches the visual cues provided. For instance, if a creator submits an image of a character, MovieGen will analyze that image to recreate the character in a video, ensuring that the character's physical appearance, clothing, and even facial expressions are faithfully reproduced. Similarly, if an image of a particular setting or background is provided, the AI will generate a video scene that mimics the textures, colors, and atmosphere of the image, effectively bringing the static photo to life.

This capability is especially useful for content creators who want to develop personalized or branded content. For example, social media influencers and marketing professionals often need to produce videos that align with a particular brand identity or aesthetic. By providing MovieGen with images that reflect their brand's look and feel—such as specific color palettes, logos, or product shots—creators can generate videos that perfectly match their visual guidelines without having to manually design every frame. This not only saves time but also ensures that the final product is consistent with their overall branding.

One real-world example of creators leveraging MovieGen's personalization feature is in the realm of personalized advertising. Companies can submit product images or customer profiles, and MovieGen can then generate personalized video ads that incorporate those images directly into the content. For instance, an e-commerce brand could provide images of their latest product line, and MovieGen would create a series of ads where these products are featured prominently in various settings, such as being used by a model or displayed in a visually appealing environment. This level of customization allows brands to target specific customer segments more effectively by delivering ads that feel personalized and relevant to individual viewers.

Another example comes from video game development, where designers use MovieGen to generate personalized cutscenes or character animations based on user preferences. By allowing players to upload images or select visual traits for their in-game characters, MovieGen can adapt the video content to match each player's unique choices. This type of personalization enhances the gaming experience by making players feel more connected to the characters they control, as the generated content directly reflects their input.

In the film industry, personalized content can also be used to cater to different cultural or regional preferences. Filmmakers can provide images of different locations, actors, or visual styles that align with the cultural nuances of various target audiences. For example, a movie scene set in one part of the world could be adapted to reflect the architectural styles, clothing, and environmental characteristics of another region, simply by feeding MovieGen the appropriate reference images. This allows filmmakers to localize their content more efficiently, tailoring it to resonate with diverse global audiences while minimizing the need for extensive reshoots or post-production edits.

The versatility of MovieGen's personalized content creation also extends to educational and training materials. Educators and instructional designers can submit images of specific tools, environments, or scenarios that are relevant to their training programs, and MovieGen can generate videos that are customized to the needs of their audience. For example, a medical training program could provide images of medical equipment or procedures, and MovieGen would generate training videos that show these tools in use, providing learners with visual content that is directly relevant to their field of study.

In conclusion, MovieGen's ability to adapt videos based on user-provided images opens up new possibilities for personalized content creation across a variety of industries. Whether for social media marketing, gaming, filmmaking, or education, the feature allows creators to produce highly customized videos that align with their specific goals and visual preferences. By streamlining the personalization process, MovieGen empowers content creators to develop tailored, engaging, and relevant content without the need for extensive manual editing, thereby expanding the potential for AI-driven creativity in the digital age.

MovieGen's generative video effects represent a major leap forward in how creators can manipulate and customize video content, offering the ability to seamlessly change backgrounds, objects, and even character appearances within a scene. These effects are not just superficial tweaks but sophisticated transformations that allow creators to control the environment, elements, and overall aesthetic of their videos with remarkable precision. By using AI to generate these changes in real-time, MovieGen opens up new possibilities for both professional filmmakers and everyday content creators.

The ability to change backgrounds is one of the most prominent features of MovieGen's generative effects. With just a simple text input or image reference, users can completely alter the setting of a video. For example, a scene originally set in a lush forest can be transformed into a windswept desert or a bustling urban landscape, all without the need to physically shoot in those locations. This capability drastically reduces the logistical challenges of location scouting, travel, and set building that filmmakers traditionally face. In one notable example, MovieGen generated a beach scene where a girl runs with a kite, and this same scene was later transformed into a desert setting, with the AI adjusting not only the background but also the lighting and atmosphere to match the new environment. The ease with which backgrounds can be swapped or altered means that filmmakers can now experiment with different visual styles and settings without costly reshoots.

MovieGen also excels in altering objects within a scene. For instance, in the earlier example of the fiery dance, where a man is holding a fiery object, the generative effects can be used to replace the fire with other objects, such as sparklers or even completely new items like glowing orbs. These changes go beyond simple object replacement; MovieGen ensures that the new objects are integrated into the scene with realistic physics, lighting, and interaction with the surrounding environment. In a more whimsical demonstration, MovieGen was able to change a runner's costume into an inflatable dinosaur suit, adding not only a visual transformation but also adjusting how the character's movements adapted to the bulkier, bouncier nature of the costume. This kind of customization opens up endless possibilities for creators looking to experiment with different props, costumes, or even fantastical elements that wouldn't be possible in a traditional film shoot.

The effects don't stop with backgrounds and objects—MovieGen also allows for environmental changes like adding or altering weather conditions. Imagine a scene originally filmed on a bright, sunny day that needs to be turned into a rainy, stormy setting for dramatic effect. MovieGen can generate realistic rain effects, including the way droplets interact with the surfaces they touch, like wetting the ground or making characters' clothing appear damp. Beyond just creating visual rain, MovieGen adjusts the entire atmosphere to suit the change, dimming the lighting, adding cloud cover, and even modifying the behavior of other elements, like wind and shadows, to create a cohesive, immersive experience. This level of detail ensures that weather changes don't feel like artificial overlays but rather like integral parts of the scene.

These generative video effects have profound implications for the film production process. Traditionally, creating effects like costume changes, weather alterations, or background replacements would require elaborate post-production work involving green screens, CGI, and significant manual input. With MovieGen, these effects can be generated and refined in real-time, reducing the time and cost associated with post-production processes. Filmmakers can experiment with different effects on the fly, making decisions about the look and feel of a scene without the need for reshooting or extended post-production timelines. This gives directors and producers more flexibility and creative freedom, allowing them to explore different artistic directions with minimal risk and effort.

For user-generated content, the impact of MovieGen's generative effects is equally transformative. Social media influencers, YouTubers, and amateur filmmakers often don't have the resources to access professional post-production tools, yet they still need polished, visually appealing content to stand out. With MovieGen, even creators with limited budgets can produce videos that rival professional productions, incorporating dynamic effects like changing backgrounds, adding visual elements, or experimenting with costume designs. Imagine a content creator shooting a vlog at home, who then uses MovieGen to change the background to a tropical beach or a futuristic cityscape—this instantly elevates the production value of their content without the need for expensive equipment or specialized editing software.

In user-generated content, another popular application of generative effects is seen in social media challenges or themed content, where creators often replicate popular trends. With MovieGen, creators can take these trends to the next level by incorporating effects like costume changes or setting transformations that make their content more engaging and visually unique. For instance, a simple dance video can be transformed with generative effects that add colorful costumes or interactive backgrounds, creating a visually stunning final product that grabs the audience's attention.

In summary, MovieGen's generative video effects—whether it's changing backgrounds, replacing objects, or adding environmental factors like rain—are revolutionizing how creators of all levels approach video production. By providing tools that allow for real-time customization and seamless integration of visual effects, MovieGen streamlines the creative process, reduces production costs, and offers new avenues for experimentation. Whether in professional filmmaking or user-generated content, the ability to manipulate and enhance video with ease empowers creators to push their creative boundaries, delivering visually rich content that was once only achievable through extensive post-production work.

Chapter 7: Video-to-Audio: The Sound Revolution

MovieGen Audio is an integral part of Meta's innovative video generation platform, designed to enhance the overall realism of AI-generated content by producing high-quality sounds that match the visual elements seamlessly. While many AI video generation tools focus on the visual aspect of content creation, MovieGen Audio goes a step further by recognizing the crucial role that sound plays in creating an immersive and believable experience. Sound is not merely an accompaniment to visuals; it significantly influences how viewers perceive a scene, affecting the mood, depth, and emotional impact of a video. MovieGen Audio's capabilities allow it to generate a wide range of realistic sounds that synchronize perfectly with the visual actions and environments presented in the video.

One of the standout features of MovieGen Audio is its ability to generate both diagetic and non-diagetic sounds. Diagetic sounds are those that come directly from the scene, such as footsteps, wind blowing, or the sound of a car engine. MovieGen Audio excels in this area by analyzing the actions and interactions within the video and generating the appropriate sounds to match. For example, in a video showing a person running across a sandy beach, MovieGen Audio would produce the sounds of footsteps crunching in the sand, the wind rustling through the air, and the distant sound of waves lapping against the shore. The system is capable of processing these inputs dynamically, ensuring that each sound is perfectly timed and corresponds with the character's movements or the environment's shifts.

In addition to diagetic sounds, MovieGen Audio is also adept at generating non-diagetic sounds, such as background music or atmospheric sound effects that aren't directly linked to the on-screen action but are crucial for setting the tone of the scene. For instance, in a tense action sequence, MovieGen

Audio might generate suspenseful music that builds intensity as the scene unfolds, even if the characters themselves are unaware of the music. This ability to blend diagetic and non-diagetic sounds enables creators to craft videos with a cinematic quality that engages viewers on both a visual and auditory level.

One of the key strengths of MovieGen Audio lies in its ability to understand the physical relationship between visual actions and the sounds they produce. For example, when generating a scene where a character jumps into water, MovieGen Audio doesn't just add a generic splash sound. It analyzes the depth of the water, the height of the jump, and the speed at which the character enters the water to produce a sound that reflects these physical dynamics. This level of detail ensures that the soundscape matches the visual cues, resulting in a more convincing and immersive experience.

Another critical feature of MovieGen Audio is its ability to generate long, coherent audio tracks for extended videos, ensuring that the sound doesn't feel repetitive or out of place. In longer scenes, such as a continuous dialogue or action sequence, MovieGen Audio can maintain consistency in ambient sounds, such as the hum of a city in the background or the subtle rustle of leaves in a forest, without looping or sounding artificial. This ability to create smooth, extended audio tracks is essential for maintaining the flow of the video and preventing any auditory distractions that could pull viewers out of the experience.

Sound matching is a vital component of achieving cinematic quality in any video production, and MovieGen Audio addresses this challenge with impressive precision. In filmmaking, sound design plays a critical role in guiding the viewer's emotional response to a scene. Whether it's the sharp crack of thunder in a dramatic storm or the subtle clink of a glass in a quiet room, the right sound at the right moment can significantly enhance the storytelling. MovieGen Audio ensures that these sounds are not only realistic but also timed perfectly with the visual action, creating a synchronized experience that feels polished and professional.

For example, in a scene where a character is holding a fiery object, MovieGen Audio would generate the crackling sounds of the fire and the faint hiss of burning fuel. These sounds would change in volume and intensity as the character moves the object around, reflecting the way sound behaves in a real-world environment. Similarly, if the fire were to flicker out or grow larger, the corresponding audio would adjust dynamically, ensuring that the sound always matches the visual representation. This level of synchronization is essential for maintaining the viewer's immersion and ensuring that the content feels believable.

The importance of sound in creating a cinematic experience cannot be overstated, and MovieGen Audio provides filmmakers and content creators with a tool that enhances the auditory dimension of their videos. Sound adds depth to visual storytelling, giving scenes a sense of place, atmosphere, and realism that visuals alone cannot achieve. With MovieGen Audio, creators can rest assured that the sounds generated for their videos will match the visual elements perfectly, adding another layer of professionalism to their work.

In conclusion, MovieGen Audio's capabilities in generating high-quality, realistic sounds make it an essential tool for any creator looking to elevate their video content. By matching sounds with visual actions and maintaining auditory consistency, MovieGen Audio ensures that every scene is as immersive and cinematic as possible. Whether producing diagetic sounds that bring on-screen actions to life or generating non-diagetic audio that sets the mood, MovieGen Audio adds a crucial layer of depth to AI-generated video content, making it an invaluable asset for filmmakers, digital creators, and content producers alike.

Sound plays a crucial role in shaping the psychological and emotional experience of video content, often influencing how viewers perceive and respond to the story unfolding on screen. In the world of film and video production, sound is typically categorized into two broad types: diagetic and non-diagetic. Both serve distinct functions in storytelling, and MovieGen's ability to generate these sounds with precision significantly enhances the overall quality and impact of AI-generated videos.

Diagetic sound refers to sounds that originate from within the story's world—sounds that characters in the scene can hear. These sounds are integral to the narrative because they anchor the audience in the environment, making the world feel more tangible and real. Examples of diagetic sound include dialogue between characters, footsteps on a gravel path, the rustling of leaves in the wind, or the sound of a car engine revving. In MovieGen, these sounds are generated based on the specific actions and interactions taking place within the scene. For instance, if a character is walking through a forest,

MovieGen will generate the crunch of leaves and twigs underfoot, along with ambient forest noises like birds chirping and wind through the trees. These sounds are intricately timed to match the character's movements, enhancing the realism of the scene.

On the other hand, **non-diagetic sound** refers to audio that does not originate from within the world of the characters, such as background music, soundtracks, or voiceovers. These sounds are added to influence the audience's emotional response or to emphasize a particular mood or theme. Non-diagetic sound can be a powerful tool in guiding how viewers feel about a scene, whether it's a suspenseful musical score building tension or soft, uplifting music accompanying a tender moment. MovieGen's capability to generate non-diagetic sounds, such as background music, allows creators to enhance the mood of their videos, making them more emotionally engaging and immersive.

The **psychological and emotional impact of sound** on video content is profound. Sound adds layers to a scene that visuals alone cannot achieve, triggering subconscious responses from viewers that shape their understanding and emotional engagement with the story. A tense musical score, for example, can make a simple, quiet moment feel ominous, while a cheerful soundtrack can transform a scene into something light-hearted and playful. The right sound at the right moment amplifies the emotional stakes of a scene, creating a deeper connection between the audience and the story.

MovieGen's ability to generate these sounds in real-time provides creators with a sophisticated tool to craft emotional depth in their videos. For example, in an action scene where a character is running through the rain, MovieGen can produce the realistic patter of raindrops, the squelch of wet shoes on pavement, and the distant rumble of thunder. These diagetic sounds not only enhance the physical environment but also contribute to the tension of the scene. Adding a layer of non-diagetic sound, such as dramatic music building in the background, increases the emotional intensity, leaving viewers on the edge of their seats.

In one example, MovieGen generated a fiery dance scene where the crackling of flames, the whoosh of fire in the air, and the rhythmic stomp of the dancer's feet on the ground were all perfectly synchronized with the visuals. These diagetic sounds ground the viewer in the moment, making the scene feel tangible and alive. At the same time, non-diagetic music was used to underscore the atmosphere, adding a pulse to the scene that elevated the drama and energy of the dance. The combination of both types of sound transformed the sequence from a mere display of movement into an emotionally charged performance.

Similarly, in a more relaxed setting like the video of the tropical sloth floating on a pool, MovieGen generated the gentle sloshing of water, the soft clinking of ice in a glass, and the faint rustling of palm trees as diagetic sounds. These details made the scene feel serene and immersive. However, the addition of non-diagetic music—slow, tropical background tunes—further enhanced the tranquil mood, guiding the audience into a state of relaxation that matched the sloth's laid-back demeanor. Without the music, the scene would still have been visually appealing, but the emotional impact would have been less pronounced.

MovieGen's ability to generate **diagetic and non-diagetic sounds** also extends to creating complex soundscapes that require multiple layers of audio. In an urban scene, for example, the AI can produce the honking of distant cars, the chatter of pedestrians, and the hum of city life, all while maintaining a cohesive auditory environment that feels authentic. At the same time, non-diagetic elements like an upbeat musical score can be layered over the diagetic sounds, contributing to the pacing and mood of the scene.

In conclusion, the psychological and emotional impact of sound is a critical element in video storytelling, and MovieGen's ability to generate both diagetic and non-diagetic sounds opens up new possibilities for creators. By matching sound effects and music with the actions, environments, and emotional tone of a scene, MovieGen helps ensure that the audience is fully immersed in the story. The combination of realistic sound effects and mood-setting background music allows creators to craft content that is not only visually compelling but also emotionally engaging, making sound an indispensable part of any video production.

Chapter 8: What MovieGen Means for Filmmakers and Creators

The film and video industry is undergoing a significant transformation with the introduction of AI-enhanced filmmaking tools like MovieGen. As these technologies become more sophisticated, they promise to revolutionize the way films, television shows, and online videos are conceived, produced, and edited. By streamlining many traditionally labor-intensive processes, AI-enhanced tools like MovieGen offer substantial benefits to both independent creators and large-scale professional productions, ushering in a new era of content creation.

MovieGen's ability to generate high-quality video from simple text inputs represents a major shift in the filmmaking landscape. Traditionally, the production of video content involves multiple steps, including writing, casting, shooting, and post-production. Each of these stages requires significant time, effort, and financial investment.

With AI-driven tools like MovieGen, many of these steps can be condensed, offering filmmakers the opportunity to rapidly generate content that would otherwise take weeks or even months to produce. By leveraging AI, filmmakers can experiment with different concepts, settings, and effects in real-time, allowing them to iterate and refine their vision without needing costly reshoots or extensive post-production work.

For independent creators, the advantages of AI-enhanced filmmaking are particularly profound. Historically, independent filmmakers and small-scale content creators have been constrained by limited budgets, which often restricts their ability to produce high-quality visual effects or shoot in multiple locations. MovieGen levels the playing field by allowing creators to generate visually stunning content without the need for expensive equipment or large crews. For example, an independent filmmaker with a limited budget could use MovieGen to simulate diverse settings—such as a bustling cityscape or a remote desert—without leaving the studio. This opens up new creative possibilities for filmmakers who were previously limited by logistical and financial constraints.

The ease of use that AI-enhanced tools like MovieGen offer is another significant benefit for independent creators. Many video production processes, such as editing, special effects, and CGI, require specialized skills and software. MovieGen simplifies these tasks, enabling creators to achieve professional-quality results with minimal technical expertise. For example, an independent creator looking to incorporate special effects, such as rain, costume changes, or dynamic lighting, can do so by simply describing what they want, and MovieGen will generate the effects automatically. This eliminates the need for complex editing software or hours spent manually adjusting each scene, allowing creators to focus more on storytelling and creativity.

Beyond its appeal to independent creators, MovieGen also offers advantages to professional filmmakers and studios. Large-scale productions often involve intricate post-production work, where visual effects, CGI, and sound design are added to the raw footage. These processes can be time-consuming and expensive, sometimes delaying the release of films or increasing production costs. MovieGen's real-time video generation capabilities allow filmmakers to experiment with different visual effects on the spot, reducing the need for lengthy post-production work. For instance, a director working on a sci-fi film might use MovieGen to visualize a futuristic city while still on set, enabling the team to make creative decisions about camera angles, lighting, and action sequences in real-time.

In addition to speeding up production timelines, AI-enhanced tools like MovieGen enable greater flexibility in storytelling. Filmmakers can quickly generate alternative versions of scenes, experiment with different character designs, or even change entire plotlines without reshooting the footage. This level of flexibility encourages more dynamic and exploratory storytelling, allowing filmmakers to push the boundaries of their narratives in ways that might not have been possible with traditional methods. For example, a filmmaker working on a fantasy film might use MovieGen to create various mythical creatures based on rough sketches or text descriptions, adjusting the design and movement of these creatures until they align perfectly with the film's aesthetic.

MovieGen also offers significant advantages when it comes to localization and personalization of content. In a globalized media landscape, many films and TV shows are localized for different markets, requiring changes in language, culture, or even specific visual elements. MovieGen can be used to rapidly generate localized versions of scenes, changing settings, characters, or even dialogue delivery to better suit regional audiences.

For instance, a film set in a Western city might be adapted to reflect the architecture and cultural norms of an East Asian location, all without needing to reshoot or manually edit the footage.

Furthermore, AI-enhanced filmmaking tools can greatly benefit the expanding world of online and user-generated content. Platforms like YouTube, TikTok, and Instagram are driven by creators who need to produce a constant stream of fresh, engaging content. MovieGen allows these creators to produce professional-looking videos quickly and with minimal effort, whether it's adding high-quality effects to a vlog or generating visually rich backgrounds for short-form videos. This democratizes video production, giving even casual creators access to tools that were once only available to professional filmmakers.

Another critical aspect of AI-enhanced filmmaking is its potential to reduce costs, particularly in terms of labor and equipment. MovieGen can generate entire video sequences, complete with realistic environments, lighting, and sound, eliminating the need for costly location shoots, set design, or specialized equipment. For filmmakers working with tight budgets, this represents a significant cost-saving measure, allowing them to allocate resources to other important aspects of production, such as casting or marketing.

Finally, AI-enhanced tools like MovieGen will likely lead to new forms of creative collaboration between human filmmakers and AI. While AI will not replace the artistic vision and direction of human creators, it can act as a powerful assistant, helping filmmakers bring their ideas to life faster and with greater precision. Directors, screenwriters, and visual artists can work alongside AI systems to generate more ambitious and visually complex content, all while retaining full control over the creative process.

In conclusion, the shift toward AI-enhanced filmmaking is poised to fundamentally change the film and video industry. Tools like MovieGen enable both independent creators and professional filmmakers to produce high-quality content more quickly, efficiently, and affordably. By streamlining workflows, reducing production costs, and offering unprecedented creative flexibility, AI is opening new doors for storytellers and content creators of all levels. As AI technology continues to evolve, its role in shaping the future of filmmaking will only grow, making it an indispensable tool for the next generation of creators.

While MovieGen and other AI-driven video technologies have made significant strides in transforming how content is created, they are not without limitations. As with any emerging technology, there are still challenges that need to be addressed, and areas where improvement is crucial for AI video tools to reach their full potential. Understanding these limitations helps set realistic expectations for the current capabilities of AI video generation and highlights the opportunities for future updates and enhancements.

One of the primary challenges faced by AI video generation systems like MovieGen is **fine-tuning the balance between creativity and technical precision**. While MovieGen excels at transforming text into video and generating impressive visual content, it can sometimes fall short when it comes to the subtleties of human creativity, such as nuanced storytelling, emotional depth, and complex character interactions. AI-generated content may struggle with capturing the intricacies of human expression, such as micro-expressions, body language, and the delicate shifts in tone that can elevate a performance from good to extraordinary. Although MovieGen is highly capable of creating visually stunning scenes, it may lack the emotional and artistic sensibilities that a human filmmaker would bring to the table.

Another limitation is **handling highly complex or abstract concepts**. While MovieGen can generate video based on straightforward prompts and scenarios, it may struggle when tasked with creating content that involves abstract themes, metaphors, or highly conceptual ideas. For instance, if a filmmaker wanted to generate a video based on an abstract concept like "the passage of time" or "the human condition," MovieGen might not interpret such prompts in a way that aligns with the creator's vision. The AI's reliance on more literal interpretations of text inputs can lead to results that feel superficial or fail to fully capture the deeper layers of meaning intended by the filmmaker. Overcoming this limitation will require further refinement in how AI models process and interpret abstract or symbolic concepts.

Rendering realistic human characters remains another area where AI video technology needs improvement. While MovieGen can produce lifelike environments, lighting, and object interactions, generating convincing human characters—especially in close-ups—continues to be a challenge. Facial expressions, skin textures, and subtle movements can still appear slightly artificial or "uncanny," detracting from the realism of the video. Achieving the high level of detail and natural fluidity required to make AI-generated human characters indistinguishable from real actors will require advances in deep learning models that focus on character modeling and animation. Improving the ability of AI to render human features and emotions with precision will be crucial for creating more immersive and relatable content.

Seamless integration of AI-generated elements with live-action footage also presents a challenge. Although MovieGen can generate entirely new video content from scratch, blending AI-generated visuals with real-world footage in a way that feels natural and cohesive can be difficult. Filmmakers often want to combine computer-generated elements with live-action scenes, but ensuring that lighting, perspective, and movement align perfectly between the two can be tricky. AI video tools must evolve to ensure better integration between digital and real-world elements, which is essential for producing films that combine practical effects with CGI. Future updates could focus on improving the seamless blending of these elements to allow for more realistic hybrid productions.

Customization and control over AI-generated content is another area that could benefit from improvement. While MovieGen provides impressive tools for generating videos based on text inputs, creators may find themselves wanting more granular control over the finer details of the content. For example, filmmakers might want to adjust specific lighting effects, tweak a character's appearance, or modify the pacing of a scene—tasks that currently require a certain degree of manual intervention. Giving creators more flexibility and control within the AI-generated framework, allowing them to fine-tune aspects of the video to their liking, will make the tool more adaptable to a wider range of creative needs.

One potential issue that needs addressing is the **risk of over-reliance on AI-driven content generation**, particularly in creative fields. As AI tools like MovieGen become more advanced and accessible, there is a concern that creators may lean too heavily on these systems, potentially stifling human creativity and innovation. While AI can assist with technical and logistical aspects of filmmaking, it should not replace the human element that drives artistic expression. Striking the right balance between utilizing AI for efficiency and maintaining the core of human creativity will be essential to ensuring that the film and video industry continues to evolve in a way that prioritizes originality and emotional depth.

Looking to the future, **predictions for improvements in MovieGen** suggest that the technology will become more sophisticated in several key areas. First, advancements in **natural language processing (NLP)** will likely enable MovieGen to better understand and interpret more complex and nuanced text inputs, allowing it to generate video content that more accurately reflects the creator's vision, including abstract or emotionally charged themes. This will open up new possibilities for filmmakers who want to push the boundaries of storytelling by using AI to visualize complex ideas and concepts.

Additionally, improvements in **deep learning models for human rendering** are expected to make AI-generated human characters more realistic, with better skin textures, more natural facial expressions, and smoother movements. As these models improve, AI tools will be able to create human characters that are virtually indistinguishable from real actors, enhancing the believability and emotional engagement of AI-generated content.

In terms of **customization and creative control**, future versions of MovieGen may offer more interactive tools, allowing creators to adjust specific aspects of the generated video directly within the AI interface. This could include sliders for controlling lighting intensity, options for adjusting camera angles, and tools for refining character movements or expressions. By giving users more control over the finer details, MovieGen can become a more versatile tool for creators who want to blend AI-driven efficiency with their unique artistic vision.

Finally, improvements in **rendering speed and efficiency** are expected to make AI-generated content production even faster, reducing turnaround times for video creation. This will benefit not only independent creators looking to produce content quickly but also large-scale productions where tight deadlines are a constant challenge. Faster rendering, combined with more advanced visual effects capabilities, will make MovieGen an even more powerful tool in the filmmaker's arsenal.

In conclusion, while MovieGen has already made significant strides in AI video generation, there are still limitations and challenges that need to be addressed. These include improving the emotional depth of AI-generated content, rendering more realistic human characters, and offering creators more control over the final output. However, as the technology continues to evolve, future updates and enhancements will likely address these issues, making AI-driven video generation an even more integral part of the film and video production process.

Chapter 9: The Future of Video Creation with AI

The long-term impact of AI-driven video generation is poised to reshape the landscape of content creation across multiple industries. As tools like MovieGen continue to evolve, they will not only streamline the process of producing high-quality video content but also unlock new creative possibilities that were previously unattainable through traditional methods. From film production to gaming, social media, and marketing, AI video tools are set to influence the next generation of content creators in profound ways, making content creation more accessible, efficient, and innovative.

In **film production**, AI-driven video generation has the potential to dramatically change how movies and television shows are made. By automating time-consuming tasks such as pre-visualization, scene generation, and special effects, AI tools can help filmmakers reduce production time and costs. This will allow creators to focus more on storytelling and artistic direction rather than getting bogged down in technical processes. AI-generated content can also be used to simulate entire scenes, characters, and environments, enabling filmmakers to explore different creative directions without committing to costly location shoots or post-production work. For example, a director working on a sci-fi film could use MovieGen to create futuristic cityscapes, alien landscapes, or complex action sequences that would otherwise require extensive CGI work, all generated in real-time with minimal effort.

The benefits of AI in film production are not limited to large studios. Independent filmmakers and small production teams will also be able to leverage AI video tools to produce high-quality content on limited budgets. AI-generated scenes, characters, and effects will allow indie creators to compete with larger studios by giving them access to professional-grade visuals without the need for expensive equipment or large teams. In the long term, this democratization of video production could lead to a more diverse range of voices in the film industry, as more creators gain the ability to bring their ideas to life.

In the **gaming industry**, AI video tools like MovieGen can revolutionize how game environments, characters, and cutscenes are developed. Traditionally, game development requires a significant amount of time and resources to create realistic worlds, animated characters, and engaging narratives. AI-driven video generation can automate many of these processes, enabling game developers to rapidly generate immersive environments and dynamic storylines based on text descriptions or input from game designers. For instance, a developer could use AI to generate entire in-game landscapes, from sprawling cities to dense forests, with AI dynamically adjusting the lighting, weather, and interactions within these environments. This would allow game creators to focus on refining gameplay mechanics and storytelling, while AI handles the heavy lifting of environment and character creation.

Furthermore, AI video generation can enable real-time, **procedural content creation** in games, allowing for more dynamic and personalized gaming experiences. Players could encounter environments, characters, and storylines that are generated on the fly, based on their actions and decisions within the game. This level of personalization and adaptability would create a more immersive and unpredictable gaming experience, where no two playthroughs are exactly the same. As AI tools continue to advance, the integration of AI-generated video content will likely become a standard feature in game development, enabling developers to create more complex and engaging worlds with less manual effort.

The impact of AI-driven video generation will also be significant in **social media and user-generated content**. With platforms like YouTube, TikTok, and Instagram serving as major hubs for video content, the demand for fresh, engaging videos is higher than ever. AI tools like MovieGen will allow content creators to produce polished, high-quality videos more quickly and efficiently. For instance, a vlogger or influencer could use MovieGen to generate eye-catching backgrounds, visual effects, or transitions that make their videos stand out from the competition. Additionally, AI-generated video content will enable creators to experiment with different formats and styles, enhancing the creative diversity of social media platforms.

One particularly exciting development in social media is the potential for **interactive and personalized content** driven by AI. Social media users may soon be able to generate personalized video content on demand, tailoring videos to their preferences or the preferences of their followers. For example, a creator could produce a video where followers can customize the background, character outfits, or even the storyline, making the content feel more interactive and engaging. AI's ability to generate unique content at scale will empower social media creators to deliver personalized experiences that keep their audiences engaged and coming back for more.

In the world of **marketing and advertising**, AI-driven video generation tools like MovieGen will open up new opportunities for personalized and targeted content creation. Brands and marketers already rely on video content as a key component of their digital marketing strategies, but producing high-quality, tailored video ads can be resource-intensive. AI tools will make it possible to generate video ads that are personalized for specific audiences based on their demographics, behaviors, and preferences. For example, a brand could use AI to create multiple versions of an ad, each with different visuals, messages, or product placements tailored to various customer segments. This level of personalization will enable marketers to deliver more relevant and engaging ads, increasing the effectiveness of their campaigns.

Moreover, AI-driven video tools will enable **real-time content generation for marketing**. Imagine a scenario where an e-commerce brand can generate a video ad that updates dynamically based on a customer's browsing history or the latest products in stock. AI could automatically generate a video featuring those products, with visuals, music, and messaging customized to reflect the customer's preferences. This ability to create personalized content on the fly will revolutionize how brands interact with their audiences, making marketing campaigns more responsive and effective.

Beyond these specific industries, AI-driven video tools will also impact broader content creation trends, such as the rise of **virtual and augmented reality**. AI-generated video content can be integrated into VR and AR experiences, creating more immersive and dynamic environments for users. For example, in a virtual reality game, AI-generated environments could evolve based on the player's interactions, creating a truly adaptive experience. Similarly, AR applications could use AI to generate real-time video overlays that enhance the user's perception of the physical world, offering new possibilities for education, training, and entertainment.

In the long term, the **fusion of AI-driven video tools with other emerging technologies** such as 5G and edge computing will further enhance the possibilities for real-time, high-quality video content creation. With faster internet speeds and more powerful computing capabilities, creators will be able to generate and distribute AI-powered video content instantaneously, expanding the reach and accessibility of these tools across industries.

In conclusion, the long-term impact of AI-driven video generation will be profound, influencing the way content is created in film, gaming, social media, marketing, and beyond. AI tools like MovieGen will streamline workflows, reduce production costs, and open up new creative possibilities for both professionals and everyday creators. As these tools continue to evolve, they will democratize content creation, making it more accessible, personalized, and innovative than ever before, while shaping the future of visual storytelling across industries.

As AI-generated content becomes increasingly advanced, there are important ethical considerations that must be addressed, particularly around issues such as deepfakes, video manipulation, and user consent. While AI tools like MovieGen offer powerful capabilities for content creation and artistic expression, they also raise significant questions about the balance between creativity and responsibility in media production. These concerns are critical in shaping how AI-generated content is developed and used, ensuring that the technology is applied ethically and transparently.

One of the most pressing ethical issues surrounding AI-generated video content is the rise of **deepfakes**—videos created using AI technology that manipulate or fabricate a person's likeness to make it appear as though they are saying or doing something they never actually did. While deepfake technology can be used for harmless or even creative purposes, such as in film or entertainment, it has also been used maliciously to spread misinformation, create non-consensual videos, or tarnish an individual's reputation. The growing sophistication of AI video tools like MovieGen means that it is becoming easier to create realistic deepfakes that are difficult to detect, which poses significant risks for privacy, security, and trust in media.

The ability to **manipulate video content** on such a granular level raises concerns about the potential misuse of AI-generated videos in both personal and public contexts. For instance, AI tools could be used to fabricate political speeches, incriminating footage, or misleading news reports, contributing to the spread of disinformation and creating confusion about what is real and what is artificially generated. In an era where digital media is the primary source of information for many people, the consequences of such manipulations could be far-reaching, undermining public trust in media and making it harder to discern truth from fiction. As AI video technology continues to advance, it is essential that safeguards are put in place to prevent the malicious use of these tools.

User consent is another critical ethical consideration when it comes to AI-generated content. The ability to create videos featuring people who have not consented to be in them, or to alter the appearance and actions of individuals without their knowledge, raises serious privacy concerns. For example, an individual's likeness could be used in a video without their permission, leading to violations of their privacy or potential harm to their reputation. The line between creative freedom and respect for individual rights becomes blurred when AI tools enable the generation of content that can manipulate reality. In this context, it is crucial for creators to obtain explicit consent from individuals whose likenesses or actions are being used or altered in AI-generated videos.

To address these ethical concerns, there must be a **balance between creativity and responsibility** in the use of AI-generated media. Creators using tools like MovieGen must recognize that while the technology offers new opportunities for storytelling and content creation, it also comes with a responsibility to use these tools ethically. This includes being transparent about when and how AI is being used, ensuring that any individuals depicted in videos have given their consent, and avoiding the creation of content that could be harmful, misleading, or invasive.

One approach to mitigating these risks is the development of **AI detection tools** that can identify whether a video has been artificially generated or manipulated. These tools could be used by platforms, publishers, or media outlets to verify the authenticity of video content before it is distributed. For example, social media platforms could integrate detection algorithms that flag deepfake content, allowing users to be informed when they are viewing AI-generated media. Additionally, media organizations could adopt ethical guidelines for the use of AI in video production, ensuring that AI-generated content is labeled clearly and that transparency is maintained throughout the production process.

Regulation and policy will also play a crucial role in addressing the ethical implications of AI-generated content. Governments and industry bodies may need to establish frameworks that govern the use of AI tools like MovieGen, ensuring that the technology is used responsibly and that individuals are protected from potential harm. For instance, laws could be enacted to require explicit consent for the use of an individual's likeness in

AI-generated videos, or penalties could be imposed for the creation of malicious deepfakes intended to deceive or harm. Regulatory measures can provide the necessary oversight to prevent the abuse of AI video tools while still allowing creators to explore the creative potential of the technology.

Despite the ethical challenges posed by AI-generated content, it is also important to recognize the **creative benefits** that these tools can offer when used responsibly. AI-driven video generation opens up new possibilities for filmmakers, artists, and content creators, enabling them to bring imaginative ideas to life in ways that were previously impossible. For instance, filmmakers can use AI tools to generate fantastical worlds or create hyper-realistic special effects without the need for extensive resources or manual labor. Artists can experiment with new visual styles, blending AI-generated elements with traditional techniques to push the boundaries of creativity. In this sense, AI tools like MovieGen can be powerful instruments for artistic innovation, as long as they are used with a sense of responsibility and awareness of their potential impact.

The challenge moving forward will be to strike the right balance between **encouraging creative exploration** and ensuring that AI-generated content does not infringe upon individual rights or contribute to societal harm. By developing ethical guidelines, promoting transparency, and establishing clear boundaries for the use of AI in video production, creators can harness the potential of AI tools like MovieGen while mitigating the risks associated with their misuse.

In conclusion, the ethical considerations surrounding AI-generated content are complex and multifaceted, involving issues of deepfakes, video manipulation, user consent, and the balance between creativity and responsibility. As AI video tools become more advanced, it is essential that creators, regulators, and platforms work together to establish ethical standards that protect individuals and maintain trust in media. With thoughtful regulation, transparency, and responsible use, AI-driven content creation can continue to thrive while respecting the rights and privacy of individuals in the digital age.

Chapter 10: Preparing for the AI-Driven Future

As AI video generation technologies like MovieGen continue to evolve and integrate into mainstream media production, creators and filmmakers must adapt to stay competitive and fully leverage the potential of these tools. Preparing for AI integration requires not only a willingness to embrace new technology but also a proactive approach to learning, experimentation, and strategic planning. For professionals to stay ahead of the curve, they must familiarize themselves with AI-driven video creation tools, understand how these technologies can enhance their workflows, and invest in resources that allow them to maximize the creative possibilities AI offers.

One of the key steps creators can take to prepare for AI integration is **learning the basics of AI-driven tools and their capabilities**. AI tools like MovieGen offer powerful features such as real-time video generation, dynamic visual effects, and automated editing—all of which can streamline the filmmaking process and enhance the quality of content. Creators should familiarize themselves with how AI tools work, including understanding how to input data (such as text or images) and how the AI interprets this data to generate video content. By gaining a solid understanding of AI's foundational principles, creators can better assess which tools are most applicable to their work and how they can integrate them into their production pipeline.

Filmmakers should also **embrace a mindset of experimentation**. AI technology is still rapidly evolving, and the best way to stay ahead of the curve is to explore its potential early. Creators should experiment with AI tools in pre-production, generating different visual concepts, testing out creative effects, and using AI for pre-visualizations to see how it can enhance their existing workflows. By incorporating AI into their process at an early stage, filmmakers can discover innovative ways to use the technology, whether that means generating virtual sets, experimenting with character design, or creating entirely new storytelling formats. Experimenting with AI tools will also help creators identify the strengths and limitations of the technology, giving them a better understanding of when and how to apply it.

To stay competitive, professionals should also invest in **AI-specific training and education**. While many filmmakers are already familiar with digital tools and software like Adobe Premiere or After Effects, AI video generation represents a new skill set that requires ongoing learning. Filmmakers and content creators can take advantage of online courses, webinars, and workshops that focus specifically on AI in media production. Many platforms, such as Coursera, Udemy, and LinkedIn Learning, offer courses on AI in creative industries, covering topics like machine learning, generative models, and natural language processing (NLP). Additionally, tech conferences and industry events often feature panels and sessions on AI-driven content creation, providing professionals with up-to-date insights and hands-on experience with the latest tools.

Building a network of **AI-savvy collaborators** is another essential step. As AI technology continues to advance, collaboration between technologists and creative professionals will become increasingly important. Filmmakers can benefit from partnering with AI developers, data scientists, and engineers who specialize in AI-driven media tools. These collaborations can lead to innovative solutions that push the boundaries of storytelling and visual effects. For example, a filmmaker working on a project with heavy CGI or virtual production needs might collaborate with an AI expert to generate realistic environments, characters, or effects more efficiently than traditional methods allow. Surrounding oneself with a community of professionals who are proficient in AI will provide filmmakers with additional support and expertise as they integrate AI into their work.

In addition to learning and collaboration, **staying informed about the latest AI developments** is crucial. AI technology is evolving quickly, with new tools, models, and capabilities being introduced regularly. Filmmakers and content creators should stay informed by following AI research, subscribing to relevant publications, and joining industry groups that focus on the intersection of AI and media production. Resources like the MIT Technology Review, TechCrunch, and Wired often cover emerging AI technologies and their impact on industries, including film and video production. Keeping up with the latest news and trends will ensure that creators are aware of cutting-edge tools and opportunities as they arise.

Investing in AI-compatible tools and software is also essential for professionals who want to integrate AI into their workflow. As AI becomes more integrated into video production, traditional software suites may not be sufficient for harnessing the full potential of AI-generated content. Filmmakers should consider investing in AI-enabled platforms that offer seamless integration with traditional editing and post-production tools. For example, tools like Runway ML, Deep Dream Generator, and NVIDIA Omniverse allow creators to experiment with AI in a user-friendly way while integrating with industry-standard software like Blender and Unreal Engine. Ensuring that the software being used is compatible with AI-driven features will help filmmakers transition smoothly as more AI tools become available.

In terms of future-proofing, creators should also consider how AI can help **streamline their production workflows**. AI tools like MovieGen have the potential to significantly reduce time spent on tasks such as location scouting, visual effects, and post-production editing. Filmmakers can use AI to automate many of these processes, enabling faster turnaround times without sacrificing quality. For example, AI can generate entire environments or background scenes that would otherwise require physical location shoots or manual CGI work. By automating these processes, filmmakers can focus more on storytelling, character development, and creative direction, while leaving the technical work to the AI.

Collaboration with AI in post-production will also become increasingly important. Editing software is already beginning to integrate AI tools that assist with tasks like color correction, sound design, and even scene selection. Filmmakers can prepare for this shift by familiarizing themselves with AI-assisted editing tools that reduce manual work while offering creative suggestions. As more post-production software incorporates AI-driven features, professionals who can work efficiently with these tools will have a significant competitive advantage.

Lastly, **anticipating the ethical and practical implications** of AI integration is crucial for filmmakers who want to use the technology responsibly. As discussed earlier, AI-driven video generation comes with ethical considerations such as deepfakes, privacy issues, and user consent. Filmmakers must ensure that they are aware of the potential risks and legal responsibilities associated with using AI, particularly when creating content that involves real people or sensitive material. Establishing ethical guidelines for AI use in video production will help filmmakers navigate the challenges that come with this new technology while maintaining creative integrity and trust with their audiences.

In conclusion, preparing for AI integration in video production requires a combination of learning, experimentation, collaboration, and staying informed. By embracing AI-driven tools, investing in education, and building a network of AI-savvy collaborators, filmmakers and content creators can ensure they remain competitive in the rapidly evolving media landscape. As AI continues to revolutionize the industry, those who adapt and integrate the technology into their workflows will be better positioned to create innovative, high-quality content that pushes the boundaries of visual storytelling.

The inevitable influence of AI on the media landscape is already becoming clear, and its transformative effects will continue to reshape how we create, consume, and interact with content. As AI-driven tools like MovieGen and others gain traction, they will introduce new workflows, empower creators with unprecedented creative freedom, and push the boundaries of what is possible in visual storytelling. The integration of AI into media production is not just a passing trend—it represents a fundamental shift in how technology can enhance creativity, streamline processes, and democratize content creation for professionals and everyday creators alike.

AI's role in transforming media can be seen across all aspects of content production. From automating technical tasks to generating high-quality visuals and sound, AI tools provide creators with the resources to produce polished, professional content at a fraction of the cost and time required by traditional methods. This democratization allows independent filmmakers, small studios, and even individual creators to access powerful technology that was once reserved for large-scale productions with vast budgets. As a result, a more diverse range of voices can emerge in the media landscape, leading to a richer, more varied array of content for audiences to enjoy.

One of the key ways AI will transform media is by **enhancing creative possibilities**. AI tools are not simply about efficiency or automation—they enable new forms of artistic expression. With the ability to generate entire environments, realistic characters, and complex visual effects from simple inputs, AI allows creators to experiment with ideas and concepts that were previously too resource-intensive to explore. Whether it's a filmmaker creating a futuristic world, a game designer generating personalized environments for players, or a social media influencer producing dynamic, eye-catching videos, AI opens up a world of possibilities that encourage experimentation and innovation.

As AI becomes more deeply integrated into content creation, it will also **redefine the boundaries between human creativity and machine intelligence**. While AI can automate many technical aspects of media production, it is the human element—imagination, emotional depth, and storytelling—that will continue to drive the most meaningful and impactful content. The role of creators will shift from performing repetitive technical tasks to focusing on high-level artistic and narrative decisions, allowing them to push the boundaries of what AI-generated content can achieve while maintaining the core of human expression.

Another major transformation AI will bring to the media industry is **personalization and interactivity**. AI's ability to generate content in real-time opens up new possibilities for interactive and personalized experiences, particularly in areas like gaming, social media, and marketing. Audiences will increasingly expect content that is tailored to their preferences, and AI will make it easier for creators to meet these expectations by producing content that adapts to individual tastes and behaviors. This shift toward personalized content will create deeper connections between creators and their audiences, making media consumption a more dynamic and interactive experience.

In addition to its creative potential, AI will have a profound impact on **efficiency and accessibility** in media production. AI-driven tools will streamline workflows, automate time-consuming processes, and reduce production costs, making high-quality content more accessible to creators with limited resources. This efficiency will benefit both large studios and independent creators, enabling faster production cycles and allowing content to be developed, refined, and distributed more quickly. As a result, audiences will have access to a wider variety of content, from blockbuster films to niche, independently produced media.

While the integration of AI into media production is inevitable, it is important to recognize that this transformation comes with challenges. Ethical considerations, such as the potential for misuse in creating deepfakes or the risk of over-reliance on AI for creative decisions, must be addressed as the technology advances. Creators, platforms, and policymakers must work together to establish guidelines that ensure AI is used responsibly and ethically, safeguarding the integrity of media content while promoting innovation.

Ultimately, the future of creativity, technology, and visual storytelling will be shaped by a **collaborative relationship between human creators and AI**. AI will not replace human creativity, but it will serve as a powerful tool that enhances the creative process, enabling creators to bring their ideas to life in new and exciting ways. By embracing AI and integrating it thoughtfully into their workflows, creators can unlock the full potential of this technology, pushing the boundaries of what media can achieve and offering audiences richer, more immersive experiences.

In conclusion, AI is set to transform the media landscape in ways that are both inevitable and exciting. From enhancing creativity and efficiency to enabling personalization and interactivity, AI will redefine how content is created and consumed. As technology and creativity continue to evolve together, the future of visual storytelling holds limitless potential—ushering in a new era of media that is more dynamic, innovative, and accessible than ever before.

Conclusion

In conclusion, Meta's MovieGen represents a major breakthrough in AI-driven video generation, offering creators and filmmakers a powerful tool to transform simple text inputs into dynamic, visually rich content. Throughout this exploration of MovieGen, several key insights emerge that highlight its potential to revolutionize video production and content creation.

One of the most significant features of MovieGen is its ability to generate high-quality, realistic videos with detailed environments, complex lighting, and sophisticated physics. Whether it's creating a fiery dance scene with dynamic lighting or generating a tranquil setting with realistic water reflections, MovieGen handles these technical elements with precision, allowing creators to produce content that rivals traditional filmmaking methods. The integration of MovieGen Audio further enhances the platform's capabilities by generating sound effects and music that match the visuals, resulting in a more immersive experience for audiences.

MovieGen also stands out for its ability to personalize content based on user inputs, such as images or specific prompts, making it an ideal tool for marketers, social media influencers, and independent filmmakers. Its capacity to modify backgrounds, alter character appearances, and seamlessly integrate generative effects like rain or costume changes opens new possibilities for creative expression and efficiency in production workflows.

However, alongside these impressive features, the rise of AI-generated content also brings important ethical considerations, including the risk of deepfakes, video manipulation, and ensuring user consent. As AI tools like MovieGen continue to develop, creators and platforms must balance the incredible creative potential of AI with the responsibility to use it ethically and transparently.

Looking to the future, it's clear that AI will continue to revolutionize video content. As tools like MovieGen evolve, they will streamline production, enhance creative possibilities, and democratize access to high-quality content creation. The next generation of video creators will have unprecedented opportunities to experiment, innovate, and produce content that pushes the boundaries of visual storytelling.

In sum, Meta's MovieGen is a pivotal step forward in AI video generation, offering a glimpse of how artificial intelligence will transform not just how we create video content but how we experience it. The fusion of creativity and technology will drive the future of media, opening new doors for creators to tell stories in ways that were once unimaginable.

www.ingramcontent.com/pod-product-compliance
Lightning Source LLC
Chambersburg PA
CBHW050308230526
45471CB00005B/2083